Unsilenced
Voices of Children Refugees

Edited and Illustrated
by
Summer Qureshi

First paperback edition February 2022

Edited by Summer Qureshi
Illustrated by Summer Qureshi

ISBN 9798424390234 (paperback)

For the children refugees who bravely shared their stories and all those who choose to listen ...

Contents

OUR VOICES OUR STORIES <u>83</u>

Acknowledgments

To the Syrian and Iraqi refugee children in my English class: Thank you. This book is for you. Teaching you English over the past two years has been my *greatest* privilege. When you were forced to leave war-torn Syria and Iraq, few of you had even reached your teenage years. One of the only things you each took with you were your stories ... stories many of you have not had the chance to share until now. Your bravery and passion inspire me every day. Although your names have been changed to protect your identities and the safety of your relatives still in Syria, you know who you are. Thank you for sharing your stories with me ... and now with the rest of the world.

I further thank the American humanitarian relief organization, The GiveLight Foundation, whose dedicated CEO/Founder Ms. Dian Alyan along with chief staff members, not only connected me with the children, but also supported this project idea unconditionally. Their devotion to refugee children reminds us of our global responsibility to help innocent boys and girls re-anchor their promising lives. This book would not have been possible without them.

In addition, I remain incredibly grateful to The Lawrenceville School in New Jersey for supporting this project through the Welles Award grant because of which I can publish this anthology after hosting numerous storytelling workshops guiding the children to use their own voices. I extend a special thanks to Lawrenceville's leading English teachers, Mrs. Bernadette Teeley and Mrs. Enithie Hunter for their invaluable advice and encouragement on this book as I shared its progress.

I would also like to extend my deepest gratitude to the translator, who like the children represented in this book, prefers to remain anonymous to protect his relatives still endangered in Syria. Once a Syrian refugee himself, he was able to re-anchor his own dreams by studying in America where he is now a physician. He mentioned my storytelling workshops with the children resonated with him deeply. I thank him for meticulously helping me translate each child's story in a way that also preserves the original Arabic words' integrity. He is the epitome of what it means to give back to your community.

Last, but not least, I want to thank my family: my mother Zahra, my father Nazer, and my sister Hanya, for believing in me and in this project since its inception. They are truly some of my biggest supporters and I could not have completed this book without their love and encouragement.

Finally, Thank YOU, for taking the time to listen ...

Introduction

A Linked Identity
By Summer Qureshi

I am from refugees of a centenarian great-grandmother
  Partitioned to Pakistan
  My living link to those born in the 1850s
Her grandma from Kabul dressed girls in youthful colors
Her father of Quraish valued women's education
Her in-laws descending from Tabrez where Shams
  enlightened Jews and Muslims
  about a cohesive heritage

I am from Central Asian, Middle Eastern relations
  But what is race?
  Just a social equation
In the midst of which I became –
  Mostly "South-Asian"
We are one human race
Still learning to embrace.

I am of immigrant parents
never expected to succeed
  he struggling in a post-war economy
  she an unwanted female devoted to learning
Yet, because of whose faith, love, and dedication
I can receive an education.

I am born in the Deep South
      Arkansas
A Little Rock Nine beneficiary –
      By-product of their brave desegregation legacy
Attending schools offering diversity.

I am of minority faith celebrated multiculturally
      henna designs on palms
      clinking *Choori* on wrists
But find community
Amongst all welcoming beliefs
Creating more than diversity –
Inclusivity.

I am from today's civil rights movements
      Seeking equality
      Slavery is over
      But seeps systemically
I am inspired by changing social dynamics –
      Fighting racial injustices
      Supporting marginalized voices
      Allying with young refugees

I am a teen supporting teens
I explore uncharted ideas fearlessly
I am the owner of my voice

History shapes who I am –
But I will shape the history I leave.

Throughout high school, I have passionately engaged with children silenced in global conflicts. My own great-grandmother's refugee narratives about the 1947 Partition remind me how children still suffer the most during crises when their safety and access to education gets compromised.

Therefore, two years ago, when I had the opportunity to teach English to Syrian and Iraqi refugee children, I felt an immense responsibility to learn from their experiences. Hoping to get to know them better, one night I asked my students to write about themselves for homework. The next day, their responses stunned me: Many children explained how much they valued family after losing a parent during the war, while others wanted to return to Syria to fight for stronger human rights despite becoming blind. They kindled the resilient spirit of the person I wanted to be, yet I along with many others rarely hear their voices. In this moment, we were inspired to work together to change the power dynamics of who *should* be heard. Using a Welles Award grant for storytelling workshops, I guided my students to write their stories from their own perspectives, now collated into this book.

My workshops focused on eight questions, reflected in the table of contents with the goal of capturing each child's unique identity based not just on their individual experiences, but more importantly on how each of them *wants* to be seen by the rest of the world. In this spirit, I hand-drew this book's custom cover depicting the mosaic tiles of one of the most beautiful mosques in Syria, the Umayyad Mosque. While these children have undergone hardship on a scale no child should have to endure, their stories serve an important reminder of the budding beauty and hope that can still emerge from challenging circumstances.

At the end of my workshops, when one young girl remarked, "Thank you for giving us a chance to share what is in our hearts," I realized our book is not an end-product but merely a stepping-stone towards changing diverse representation... which can only exist when we give children the chance to speak for themselves and when we ourselves take the time to listen.

You are about to hear the raw stories of refugee children who take ownership of their own identities, giving a voice not just to their stories, but also to their futures. Many children still have family at risk in Syria, so to protect themselves and their families, the names in this book have been changed. Still, the essence of each child is preserved as I chose names whose meanings encapsulate each child's personality. Similarly, I have intentionally designed illustrations representing each child's dreams. *This* is how the children hope to be seen.

Lastly, before reading their stories, I think it is important to remember that no matter one's background or personal beliefs, we are all linked. We are linked not only by our history, but also by our choice to interact and listen to one another's experiences. By reading their stories, you are now linking part of your identity with these brave, young refugee children...

Who Am I to Me?

Who am I to me?

Recapturing our Childhood

Shuja – Boy, Age 15

Hazeem – Boy, Age 20

Jehaan – Girl, Age 13

Ameed – Boy, Age 14

Farrah – Girl, Age 13

Raja – Girl, Age 12

Taliha – Girl, Age 13

Munira – Girl, Age 10

Mahir – Boy, Age 17

Azeema – Girl, Age 11

Aqsa – Girl, Age 12

Iman – Girl, Age 12

Who am I to me?

شجا

انا سوري. انا عمري
١٥ و احب الغامرة و
المخاطرة

Who am I to me?

Shuja - Brave

I am Syrian. I'm 15 years old. I love adventure and taking risks

Who am I to me?

هزيم

أنا من سورية دمشق. عمري
عشرون سنة. أعمل وأدرس
في نفس الوقت، وأريد أن
أصبح شخصاً قادراً على
مساعدة مجتمعه وبلده

Hazeem - Intelligent

I'm from Damascus, Syria. I'm 20 years old. I'm working and studying at the same time, and I want to be someone who can help his community and his homeland

Who am I to me?

جيهان

لا تأثر الحرب وأسباب الهجرة على هدفنا بالحياة في الحياة

Who am I to me?

Jehaan - Creative

The war and the reasons to migrate do not affect our goal in life

14

Who am I to me?

عميد

انا عميد من سورية غلام
مسلم.
أحب المدرسة والرياضة
وأحب أن أتعلم اللغات

Who am I to me?

Ameed - Leader

I am Ameed from Syria, a
Muslim boy.
I love school, sports, and
I like to learn languages

فَرَح

أنا سوريّة. أنا تلميذة. أعمل
بجد

Farrah - Happiness

I am Syrian. I am a student. I am hard-working

رجاء

أنا شخص إيجابي. أنا جميلة
وسعيدة

Who am I to me?

Raja - Hope

I am a positive person. I am beautiful and happy

Who am I to me?

طليحة

أنا عميقة التفكير

Who am I to me?

Taliha - Curious

I am thoughtful

منيرة

انا منيرة ... فتاة الحرب... فتاة
الحصار... فتاة
الحرية ... سأكبر واتعلم واحقق
حلمي واعود إلى بلدي

Munira - Full of Light

I'm Munira ... A girl of war ... A girl of siege ... A girl of freedom ... I will grow up, learn, achieve my goal, and return to my homeland

ماهر

أنا عمري سبع عشرة سنة.
قَدِمْتُ إلى تركيا من ستِّ سنين.
مَرَرْتُ بمرحلة صعبة في البداية
لأنّني لم أعرف اللغة التركية

Mahir - Skillful

I'm 17 years old. I came to Turkey 6 years ago and I was going through a difficult period at first because I didn't know Turkish

Who am I to me?

عظيما

أحب الدراسة وأن أبقى في اسطنبول وأن لا نتغرّب لبلد ثانٍ وأن أتعلّم وأن أصير معلمة في المستقبل

27

Azeema - Determined

I want to study, stay in Istanbul, not get deported to another country, learn, and become a teacher in the future

Who am I to me?

أقسى

أحلم بأن أصبح عالمة
فيزياء طبيعية

Who am I to me?

Aqsa - Intelligent

I dream of becoming a physicist

إِيمَان

اريد ان أكون فتاة وردية
مليئة بالطاقة والإيجابية وأريد
ان اصنع شيء إيجابي في
مجتمعنا

31

Iman - Faith

I want to be a pink optimistic girl full of energy and positivity, and I want to do something positive in my community

What Does it Mean to Be a Refugee?

What does it mean to be a refugee?

Recapturing our Childhood

Shuja – Boy, Age 15

Hazeem – Boy, Age 20

Jehaan – Girl, Age 13

Ameed – Boy, Age 14

Farrah – Girl, Age 13

Raja – Girl, Age 12

Taliha – Girl, Age 13

Munira – Girl, Age 10

Mahir – Boy, Age 17

Azeema – Girl, Age 11

Aqsa – Girl, Age 12

Iman – Girl, Age 12

What does it mean to be a refugee?

شجا

كل من ينفصل عن بلده يشعر أن مكانه ليس هنا بل مكانه في بلده. يشعر أنه في المكان الخطأ

What does it mean to be a refugee?

Shuja - Brave

Everyone who leaves his homeland feels that this is not his place, but rather his place is in his homeland. He feels like he is in the wrong place

What does it mean to be a refugee?

هزيم

تعني أنّك لا تملك حقوقاً مثل غيرك

What does it mean to be a refugee?

Hazeem - Intelligent

It means that you do not have rights like others

What does it mean to be a refugee?

جيهان

نحن نعاني من موضوع اللغة التركية. لا نستطيع تعلم اللغة التركية

What does it mean to be a refugee?

Jehaan - Creative

We are suffering because of the Turkish language. We cannot learn the Turkish language

What does it mean to be a refugee?

عميد

انا سوري ولا عرف سورية.
خرجت من سورية كنت صغيراً.
لا أعرف معنى لاجئا لكن أريد أن أعيش في وطني

What does it mean to be a refugee?

Ameed - Leader

I'm Syrian but I don't know Syria. I left Syria when I was a little kid. I don't know the meaning of refugee. However, I want to live in my homeland

42

What does it mean to be a refugee?

فَرَح و رجاء

يعني أنا أعيش في
تركيا، لكنني سوري

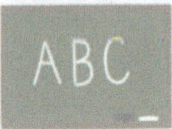

43

What does it mean to be a refugee?

Farrah - Happiness and Raja – Hope

It means I live in Turkey, but I am Syrian

What does it mean to be a refugee?

طليحة

تعني أن عدم معرفتك أي شيء عن بلدك. تعني أن تعاني من العنصرية تجاهي وتجاه اللاجئين السوريين

What does it mean to be a refugee?

Taliha - Curious

It means not knowing about my country. It means experiencing racism towards me and other Syrian refugees

What does it mean to be a refugee?

منيرة

نحن لسنا لاجئين عند أحد...
نحن ضيوف وسنعود إلى بلادنا
يوما ما... لانعرف متى لكن
حتما سنعود

What does it mean to be a refugee?

Munira - Full of Light

We are not refugees ... we are guests and one day we will return to our homeland ... We don't know when, but we're definitely going back

ماهر

أشتاق لبيتي كثيراً. كَوْني لاجئ يجعلني غريباً في هذه البلد. لا أتأثّر بالتعليقات السلبية لأنّني فقط أنظر إلى أهدافي

What does it mean to be a refugee?

Mahir - Skillful

I just miss my home. Being a refugee makes me a stranger to this country. I am not affected by negative comments because I just look at my goals

What does it mean to be a refugee?

عظيما

تعب نفسي
كلمة لاجئا لا أحبها لاني انا
وعائلتي مجبورين للجوء.
لاأستطيع لعودة الى بلدي

What does it mean to be a refugee?

Azeema - Determined

Mental exhaustion. I don't like
the word 'refugee' because my
family and I are forced to
become refugees. I can't go
back to my homeland

What does it mean to be a refugee?

أقسى

نحن نتمنى أن نعيش بسلام
ونتعلم لكن لست مرتاحة

What does it mean to be a refugee?

Aqsa - Intelligent

We hope to live in peace and to learn, however, I'm not comfortable

What does it mean to be a refugee?

إِيمَان

نحن لسنا لاجئين
باستطاعتنا نحن فقط
أجبرنا بسبب الحرب

What does it mean to be a refugee?

Iman - Faith

We're not refugees by choice.
We were just forced because of
the war

Who Do I Want to Be in the Future?

Who do I want to be in the future?

Recapturing our Childhood

Shuja – Boy, Age 15

Hazeem – Boy, Age 20

Jehaan – Girl, Age 13

Ameed – Boy, Age 14

Farrah – Girl, Age 13

Raja – Girl, Age 12

Taliha – Girl, Age 13

Munira – Girl, Age 10

Mahir – Boy, Age 17

Azeema – Girl, Age 11

Aqsa – Girl, Age 12

Iman – Girl, Age 12

شجا

محامي الذي يدافع عن حقوق الناس ويساعد الضعفاء، أو تاجر الذي يساعد الناس بأموالهم

Who do I want to be in the future?

Shuja - Brave

A lawyer who defends people's rights and helps the weak or a merchant who helps people with their money

Who do I want to be in the future?

هزيم

شخصا رائعا مثل أمي

61

Who do I want to be in the future?

Hazeem - Intelligent

Someone great like
my mom

Who do I want to be in the future?

جيهان

حلمي ان اكون من المشاهير الكبار.
احلم بمستقبل جيد. احلم بأن أصبح ممثلة

Who do I want to be in the future?

Jehaan - Creative

My dream is to become one of the most famous celebrities. I dream of a good future. I dream of becoming an actress

Who do I want to be in the future?

عميد

أريد أن أكون قائدا

Who do I want to be in the future?

Ameed - Leader

I want to be a leader

Who do I want to be in the future?

فَرَح

هدفي أن أصبح دكتور
وأساعد عائلتي

Who do I want to be in the future?

Farrah - Happiness

My goal is to be a doctor and help my family

رجاء

أريد أن أصبح مدير روضة الأطفال

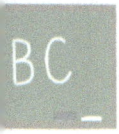

Who do I want to be in the future?

Raja - Hope

I want to be a principal for kindergarteners

Who do I want to be in the future?

طليحة

هدفي الوحيد في الحياة هو السعادة في المستقبل وأن أكون أفضل مصمّم أزياء

Who do I want to be in the future?

Taliha - Curious

My only goal in life is my future happiness and to be the best fashion designer

Who do I want to be in the future?

منيرة

اريد ان اكون كاتبة

73

Who do I want to be in the future?

Munira - Full of Light

I want to be a writer

Who do I want to be in the future?

ماهر

أريد أن أصبح مهندساً معمارياً أو مهندس حاسوب

Who do I want to be in the future?

Mahir - Skillful

I want to be an architect or a computer engineer

Who do I want to be in the future?

عظيما

أحب الدراسة وأحب أن أتعلم اللغة التركية بسرعة وأن أصبح معلمة

Who do I want to be in the future?

Azeema - Determined

I like to study, and I like to learn Turkish quickly and become a teacher

Who do I want to be in the future?

أقسى

اريد ان اكون عالمة فيزياء

Who do I want to be in the future?

Aqsa - Intelligent

I want to be a physicist

Who do I want to be in the future?

إِيمَان

سوف أبني بناءً كبيراً للدورات التعليمية، للبنات وللتسوّق، وفندق حيث يمكنهن تعلّم أيّ شيء يحبوه. معظم الأماكن للرجال، لذلك أريد أن أصنع عالم وردي للبنات

Who do I want to be in the future?

Iman - Faith

I will build a big building for girls for educational courses, shopping, and a hotel where they can learn. Most places are for men, so I want to make a pink world for girls

Our voices. Our stories.

Our
Voices
Our
Stories

Our voices. Our stories.

Recapturing our Childhood

Shuja – Boy, Age 15

Jehaan – Girl, Age 13

Ameed – Boy, Age 14

Taliha – Girl, Age 13

Munira – Girl, Age 10

Mahir – Boy, Age 17

Azeema – Girl, Age 11

Aqsa – Girl, Age 12

Jasira – Girl, Age 15

شجا

بدأت الحرب في سوريا في عام ٢٠١١ في شهر آذار.
كان عمري ٤ سنوات وبالرغم من صغر سني حينها إلا أنني
كنت أعي وأفهم بعض ما كان يدور حولي. أذكر عندما بدأت الحرب
في بلدنا كان معظم الشباب والنساء يخرجون في الشوارع ويطالبون
بالحرية كما كنا نسمعهم يهتفون...

تسارعت الأحداث وبدأ قصف الطيران وبدأت الطائرات
برمي الصواريخ على المنازل والاحياء لتدمرها وكنا نختبئ عند
القصف خائفين من صوت الطائرات العالي واستمر هذا الحال أياماً.

ولم يصدق العالم ما حدث عندما تم القصف بالسلاح الكيماوي هناك
مئات الأطفال والنساء يختنقون بهذه المادة السامة. أطفال ميتة ونساء
تصرخ وكل من حولنا يسعل ويختنق. كنا نهرب للسطح لأن الغازات
السامة تكون قاتلة في الشوارع والمنازل في الطوابق الاولى من
الأبنية.

لا أعلم تماما كيف بقينا أحياء وقتها ولكن الأيام تمضي والقصف
يستمر...أذكر أول خروج لنا من منزلنا حيث هجرنا منزلنا الجميل
و ألعابي في الغرفة سيارتنا الصغيرة قرب المنزل و دكان والدي في
الحي. تركنا كل ما كان لنا يوماً لنحمل العناء والمأساة ونحن ننتقل

85

من مكان إلى مكان هربا من الموت والقصف والجنود باحثين عن ملجأ نشعر فيه بالأمان.

حتى وصلنا بلدة سمعتهم يسمونها عدرا. كان أبي يبحث لنا عن منزل نعيش فيه معا عندما اعتقله جنود النظام دون أي تهمة سوى أنه قادم من الغوطة. أبي كان يمنحنا الأمان بلمسة يديه عند الخوف من الطائرة. أبي كان يحملني لنخرج مسرعين عند القصف، فمن سيحملني إن أخذه الجنود؟

كانت تلك الأسئلة تدور في رأسي وأنا أسمع أمي تحاول الحصول على أي معلومة عنه ليصلها خبر أنه على قيد الحياة أم أنهم قتلوه ... كانت أمي تسأل عن والدي في الفترات الأولى من الاعتقال دون خبر عنه.

بقينا مع جدي وجدتي لفترة قصيرة ولكن ضيق الحال وقلة المال. أجبر أمي باتخاذ قرار العودة للغوطة لبيتنا لذكرياتنا مع أبي الحبيب. كنت في الصف الأول أذهب إلى المدرسة يوماً أو يومين فقط كل أسبوع خوفا من القصف في باقي الأيام.

مع مرور الايام أصبحنا نميز انواع القذائف التي تتساقط فوق بيوتنا الصواريخ أو البراميل أم غيرها... كان الجامع قريباً من بيتنا وكنا نشعر فيه بالأمان والسكون. نذهب هناك لنحفظ القرآن الكريم ونتعلم اللغة العربية بالرغم من كل القصف حولنا.

أذكر جيدا شعور الرعب والخوف الشديد عند مشاهدتي للجرحى و الأشلاء على الطرقات ولم يكن والدي معي ليمسكني فقد اعتقله الجنود وحرموني من الأمان .... تقول أمي أنني كنت أبكي أن صادفنا رجلا يشبه أبي في الطريق أقف وأتأمل حركاته...وأتمنى لو كان أبي معي الذي كان سندي وأماني.

ثم بدأ الحصار وكنا نعيش بلا كهرباء وقلّ الطعام والماء حتى صرنا نشتهي الخبز أو الحلوى، كانت الأمهات يصنعن لنا خبز الشعير وعلف الحيوانات ليسد جوعنا كما أكلنا الملفوف بدلا من الخبز كنا نشتهي الأرز والفواكه والبيض لم نشبع أبداً كل ليلة وكل صباح كل ماحدث هناك لا يصدق ولكننا عشناه. سنروي تلك الايام الصعبة التي قضيناها كالاموات بكل أوجاعها وآلامها وقصفها، حتى الماء كنت أجلبه لوالدتي عن طريق بئر في الأرض عن طريق الضخ بأنوب صغير كنت متعباً وصغيراً ولكني رجل المنزل كما قالت امي ويجب أن اساعدها.

كانوا يؤمنون بعض الكهرباء عن طريق المولدات الكهربائية لمدة ساعة أو ساعتين لا أكثر مع العلم أن كل هذه الأشياء كانت باهظة الثمن جدا، نحن اطفالٌ مظلومون وأنا لا أحب الظلم كانت أمي تتلو علينا أية من القرآن الكريم (إن الله لا يحب الظالمين)، الظلم ليست كلمة نكتبها. الظلم لا يعرفه إلا من عاشه وشعر به ظلم حرماننا من الأب وظلم الخوف الذي كنا نعيشه خلال ٢٤ ساعة في كل يوم ليلا ونهارا وظلم حرماننا الأمان، ظلم الأطفال الأبرياء المشردين في والطرقات والأزقة الذين لا يجدون ملجأ وفقدوا والديهم وهم الآن

Our voices. Our stories.

أيتام ظلم الجوع الذي مررنا به في كل تلك السنين وحتى الآن هناك من يعيشه في بلدي الحبيب.

كنا نعد الأيام بانتظار خبر عن أبي المعتقل في السجون ... المظلمة...حتى جاء اليوم الموعود وبفضل من الله عاد إلينا والدي ولكن ليس بصحته. الجيدة فأصابه مرض السرطان خلال فترة اعتقاله وإلى الآن ما يزال يتعالج وبالرغم من كل هذه الأشياء التي كنا نعيشها إلى أننا لم نستسلم وبعد فترة قصيرة من خروج والدي من السجن قررنا أن نغادر من بلدنا إلى تركيا من أجل علاج والدي وأيضا لكي نهرب من ظلم النظام لنا... وسافرنا الى تركيا والحمد لله أنها بلد إسلامية وجميلة حيث وجدنا الأمان الذي كنا بحاجة إليه في بلدنا.

والحمد لله تابعت دراستي وحفظي للقرآن الكريم فهناك الكثير من المعاهد الشرعية. أنا الآن أدرس و أعمل في فترة الصيف لكي أساعد والدي في مصروف المنزل. الآن أنا شاب طموح في الخامسة عشر من عمري وأتمنى أن أصبح تاجرا والآن أشتري وأبيع أخسر وأربح وكل ذلك من جهدي وتعبي.

Shuja - Brave

The war started in March 2011 in Syria. I was 4 years old. Even though I was a young kid then, I was a aware of what was going on around me. I remember many guys and women going out to streets demanding freedom when the war started in our country. We used to hear them cheering ...

By then, events accelerated, and the shelling started. War planes started to fire rockets towards houses and towns, destroying them. We used to hide during the shelling, scared of the very loud noises. This situation lasted for days.

The world didn't believe that chemical weapons were used against us. Hundreds of children and women were suffocating because of this poison. Dead kids and shouting women ... everyone around us was coughing and suffocating. We were running away to rooftops because the poisonous gas was deadly in the streets and in the first floors of the buildings.

Our voices. Our stories.

I don't know exactly how we stayed alive then. Days passed and the shelling continued... I remember that the first time we left our house, I left my toys in my room ... we left our small car close to the house ... we left my father's store. We left everything behind, and instead carried sufferings and tragedy as we moved from one place to another, running away from death, shelling, and the soldiers, looking for a refuge to feel safe.

Finally we reached a town that was called Adra. My father was looking for a house for us when the regimen soldiers arrested him without having any charge except that he was originally from Al-Ghouta. My father used to give us a sense of safety when we were afraid of war planes. My father used to carry me when we left in a hurry during the shelling. Who would do that if the soldiers took him?

Those questions circulated in my mind while I listened to my mother trying to get any information about him, wondering if he was still alive or dead... my mother was asking about my father during the early stages of his arrest, but there was no answer...

We stayed with my grandparents for a short while, however, due to the difficult situation and the shortage of money, my mom decided to return to Al-Ghouta ... to our home ... to our memories with my lovely father. I was in first grade. I used to go to school once or twice a week because there was scary shelling during the other days.

As days passed by, we started to recognize the different types of shelling and bombs that fell over our houses. The mosque was close by our house. We used to feel safe there. We go there to memorize the Holy Quran and learn the Arabic language, despite the shelling around us.

I remember the intense fear I felt when I saw the wounded people and the massacred body parts in the streets. My father was not with me because he was arrested. They took the person who gave me a sense of safety. My mother says that I cried when we met a guy on the road who looked like my father and that I stopped to watch him carefully. I wished my father was with me. He was my safety.

Then the siege started. We were living without electricity. We didn't have enough food or water. We were craving bread and desserts. Mothers used to make bread from barley and fodder to ease our hunger. We ate cabbage instead of bread. We were craving rice, fruits, and eggs. We never felt full every night and every morning. Everything that happened then was unbelievable. However, we survived. We will tell stories about those difficult days when we lived like dead people with all the pain, the suffering, and the shelling. I used to bring water to my mother from a well connected to a small pump. I was young and very tired, but I also was the man of the house as my mother said, and I had to help her.

They were supplying us with some electricity via electric generators for an hour or two a day, however, this was very expensive. We were oppressed children. I don't like oppression. My mother recited us a verse from the Holy Quran (Allah [God] does not like the oppressors). Oppression is not just a word we write.

Our voices. Our stories.

No one can understand oppression except the ones who experienced it. We lost our father. We felt oppression and fear 24/7, every day and night. We didn't have safety. All those homeless kids in the streets, who didn't have a refuge, who lost their parents and were orphans, faced oppression too. We faced the opression of hunger over the years, and even now, there are still people living it in my lovely country.

We were counting the days, waiting to hear news about my arrested father in the dark prisons. Until one day, thank God, he came back to us. However, he wasn't healthy. He got cancer during his arrest time. He is still getting treatment. Despite all of this, we have not surrendered. Some time after my father was released, we decided to leave our country to Turkey for my father's treatment and to escape the oppression of the regime ... we traveled to Turkey. Thank God, it's a beautiful Muslim country where we found safety that we missed in our country.

Thank God, I continued my education and I continued memorizing the Holy Quran because there are many Islamic institutes. Now I'm studying and working during the summer to help my father make income. Now, I'm an ambitious guy, 15 years old, and I hope to become a merchant. I will buy and sell, win and lose. I will do my best.

جيهان وأقسى

انا جيهان واختي أقسى.

كنا نعيش في بيتنا بدمشق.

كانت الحياة طبيعية نوعا ما حتى بدأت الحرب وخرج الناس ببعض المظاهرات للمطالبة بحقوقهم المسلوبة.

عندها بدأت الطائرات تقصف البيوت والجنود تطلق الرصاص بشكل مباشر باتجاه المتظاهرين وبسبب موقع منزلنا في السوق الشعبي... كنا شاهدين على مقتل المتظاهرين وكانت أمي تصعد بعد الاشتباكات على السطح لتجمع فوارغ الرصاصات وتفقد أحجامها... المختلفة حيث كان بعضها طويلاً يتجاوز العشرسنتيمترات.

كنا ننزل لأسفل الدرج لنختبئ من رصاصات الهيلوكبتر وقذائف ال F16 كما كنت اسمع من الناس حولي... حاول السكان إصلاح منازلهم المتضررة كل مرة بعد هدوء القصف بقدر ما يستطيعون ولكن دخول الجيش وتفتيشه البيوت كان الأكثر رعباً لنا... رغم أنهم كانوا يبحثون عن أشخاص وشباب محددين بالاسم.

وبعد أيام بدأ الحصار ليمنع الناس من الدخول للحي أو الخروج منه مع القصف المستمر دون كهرباء أو ماء أو طعام... بدأ الجيران يتقاسمون ما لديهم من طعام ليسدو جوع أطفالهم واستمر هذا الحال حتى بدأ الجيش بما يسمى الضربة الكبرى ورغم اختباء الناس في أقبية

الأبنية... إلا أن الصواريخ حصدت أرواح الكثيرين ممن كانوا يتراكضون هاربين وبعد هدوء القصف حاولنا الخروج رغم تهدم البناء والدرجات... خطونا بحذر حتى خرجنا لنشاهد مناظر لا تنسى.

البيوت مدمرة والناس قتلى كل يصرخ باسم قريبه أو جاره ولكن هل من مجيب... خرجنا من الحي لنسكن مع بيت جدي لمدة عامين... رغم وجود بعض القذائف لكن الوضع كان أفضل من الحصار والجوع حتى استطاعت أمي أن تدبر أمر سفرنا لتركيا... حيث بدأنا نتعلم اللغة وندرس في المدارس ونمارس هوايتنا المفضلة وهي الرسم.

Jehaan - Creative and Aqsa - Intelligent

I'm Jehaan, and my sister is Aqsa.

We used to live in our house in Damascus. It was somehow a normal life until the war started, and the people went out in protests demanding their stolen rights.

When the war planes started shelling the houses, the soldiers began shooting directly at the protesters. Because our house was in a popular market... we witnessed the death of protesters, and my mother used to go up to the roof after the clashes to collect the empty bullets examining their different sizes. Some of them were long, exceeding 10cm.

We used to go downstairs to hide from the bullets. I would hear people talking about the helicopter and the F16 shells... people tried fixing their damaged houses as much as they could after the silence of the bombardment. However, the scariest part was when the army entered and searched our houses ... even though they were looking for specific men by name.

After several days of siege that prevented people from entering or leaving the town, continuous shelling, and no electricity, water or food, our neighbors started sharing their leftover food to feed the children. This situation lasted until the army made their big move. Even though people were hiding in their basements, the rockets killed so many lives of those who were running away. After the shelling calmed down, and despite the destruction, we stepped outside and saw unforgettable scenes ...The houses were destroyed, and the people were dead. Everyone was shouting the names of his/her relatives or neighbors, however, there was no answer.

We left our town to live with our grandfather for 2 years. Despite some shelling, it was a better than the siege and hunger. Finally, my mother was able to arrange for us to travel to Turkey where we started learning the language, studying at schools, and practicing my favorite hobby which is drawing.

Our voices. Our stories.

عميد

اسمي عميد من سورية ولدت في حلب.

لا أذكر تفاصيل من سنوات عمري الأولى ولكن يقال عني كنت طفلاً ذكياً. بدأت الحرب في سورية وأنا في الثالثة من عمري لم أكن أفهم ماذا يحدث حولي إلا أنها كانت أصوات مخيفة، قلق عائلتي والخوف في نظراتهم غالبا ما كانت تزيد من خوفي... بعد فترة من تساقط القذائف والقنابل على قريتنا.

تركنا بيتنا وذهبنا إلى قرية أخرى في نفس المحافظة لنبعد عن أصوات القنابل ولأن كل الناس خرجت للخلاء لتفادي هدم البيوت فوق رؤوسهم، كان الجميع يقضي لياليه في الشوارع ينام ويستيقظ، في الشارع لعدة أيام وكلما اشتد القصف على قرية تخرج الأهالي للقرية التي تليها للبحث عن الأمان. وبقينا على هذه الحال ما يقارب أربعة أو خمسة أشهرٍ... ولما تساوت جميع القرى بالقصف و أصبحت كل حلب تقصف بالقنابل والطائرات.

توقفنا عن الهرب و عدنا الى بيتنا لنواجه مصيرنا...
كنا ننام على أصوات طائرات ونستيقظ على أصوات الانفجارات.

99

تقول أمي في ذاك الوقت ورغم صغر سني   كنت كلما ذهبت لفراشي انادي أخواتي وأمي لنجتمع تحت غطاء الفراش عله يحمينا من الأصوات المخيفة، لم أدرك وقتها أن هذه الأصوات هي صواريخ يمكن أن تهدم البيت كاملا فوق رؤوسنا ورغم القصف المستمر على المدينة عاد كل الناس إلى بيوتهم و فتح الباعة دكاكينهم.

وأنا بدأت أتعلم القراءة والكتابة مع أستاذ كنا كنت أكتب الحروف والارقام، وأحفظ بعض السور من القرآن الكريم ،كنت أذهب إلى أستاذي صباحا وعندما أعود أذهب مع جدي لرعي الأغنام.

حتى بلغت عمر الرابعة أو أكثر بأشهر و في ليلة من الليالي التي تخلو من صوت القصف على غير العادة... فالعادة أن أصوات القصف لا تهدأ ولكن تلك الليلة كانت هادئة تماماً.

غفونا على ذلك الهدوء لنستيقظ منتصف الليل على أصوات انفجارات ضخمة لم أسمعها من قبل، كانت من أطول الليالي وكأنها عام كامل.

وفي الصباح خرجنا من البيت لنر نصف الحي قد قصف ودمر و مئات الأشخاص قد قتلوا بالقصف العنيف. 12من اقربائنا كانوا جثثاً لا تتحرك... كانوا موتى حقاً دون روح ولشدة الرعب الذي سقط على عيني من مشاهدة مناظر القتل والموت يومها.

Our voices. Our stories.

فقدت 90% من بصري ولم أعد أستطيع الرؤية جيداً كان خوفاً لا يمكن وصفه... بعد تلك الحادثة لم أعد قادراً على القراءة أو التعلم فأنا شبه فاقد للبصر وبدأت عائلتي تبحث لي عن علاج ليعود بصري. كنت أسافر من منطقة الى أخرى مع أبي وجدي للبحث عن طبيب.

وبعد عدة أيام وجدنا طبيباً وبعد المعاينة قال لا أستطيع أن أفعل شئ. يجب بعض الصور والتحاليل ولا يوجد مشفى يعمل فكل المشافي قصفت.

لم يبقى أمام أبي إلا أن نذهب لتركيا للعلاج.
أذكر ذلك اليوم كان من أصعب الأيام أيضا.
دخلنا انا وعائلتي الحدود التركية نركض في الظلام. كنت أسمع اصوات الرصاص وبكاء إخوتي ولا أرى أمامي سوى القليل من نور الشمس... عبرنا الحدود.

ووصلنا إلى إسطنبول. استأجر أبي منزلاً فارغا دون سجاد او مدفئة لا فراش ولا شيئ فيه كان وقت الشتاء والثلج يغطي المدينة الواسعة لم يبقى مع أبي مال ليشتري طعام أو أغطية او أي شيء من أثاث. للمنزل كنا نشعر بالبرد الشديد لعدة أيام ولكن طرق باب المنزل بعض الأتراك ومعهم القليل من الأثاث.

كانوا من أحسن الناس معنا. تعرفنا على سيدة تركية ذهبت معي انا وأمي إلى المشفى للعلاج لأن أمي لا تتكلم اللغة التركية وبعد عدة أشهر

101

من ذهابنا إلى المشفى وظهور التحاليل قال الطبيب لا يوجد علاج فحالتي لا علاج لها.

لكن يجب أن أذهب إلى المدرسة.
خضعت للعلاج النفسي لمدة عام.
وبمساعدة الإخوة الأتراك تعلمت اللغة التركية وأنا الآن في الصف الخامس.

نواجه بعض المواقف العنصرية أحيانا كقول سيدة لي انا وأخوتي ونحن نلعب أحدى ايام العيد، اذهبوا إلى سورية... خربتم بلدكم والآن تريدون تخريب تركيا... لم أعلم ماذا أجيب فابتسمت ودخلت المنزل. نواجه كل يوم غلاء الأسعار والأجارات المرتفعة للبيوت. عائلتنا تتكون من ستة أشخاص وتعيش في منزل صغير... لكنه كبير بأحلامنا.

سأحقق حلمي عندما أكبر و أكون قائداً أحمي وطني وأساعد كل الفقراء والمساكين ولكن حتى اليوم لم أفهم لماذا توجد الحروب؟ وما ذنبي أن أفقد بصري؟ ما ذنب الأطفال الذين قتلوا؟! ربما يوماً سيعود بصري وسنعود للوطن ولمنزلنا الكبير هذا أملي...

Our voices. Our stories.

Ameed - Leader

My name is Ameed. I'm from Syria. I was born in Aleppo. I don't remember details of my first few years, but I was told that I was a smart kid. The war started in Syria when I was 3 years old. I didn't understand what was happening around me, but I remember scary loud noises and my family's fear which increased my fear.

As the shelling continued in our village, we left our house and went to another village in the same governorate to be away from the shelling noise. All the people went outside to avoid the possible rubble of their homes from falling on their heads. Everyone spent the nights in the streets, sleeping and waking up there for several days. Every time the shelling intensified in one village, people left to another village seeking safety… we remained in this situation for about 4-5 months. However, when shelling reached all the villages equally, and all of Aleppo was being bombed, we stopped running away, and we returned to our home to face our fate.

Our voices. Our stories.

We used to sleep to loud plane noises and wake up to the sounds of bombs. My mother said during that time, even though I was very young, when I went to bed, I called my siblings and my mother to gather under the mattress cover, thinking it might protect us from the scary noises. I didn't realize then that those rockets I heard might destroy the entire house over our heads.

Despite the continuous shelling over the city, people returned to their homes and opened their stores. I started learning how to read and write with my teacher. I wrote down letters and numbers, and memorized verses from the Holy Quran. I would visit my teacher in the morning, and I would help my grandfather herd the sheep when I returned.

When I was about 4 years old, during one unusually quiet night, we slept peacefully, only to wake up at midnight to intense bombing sounds we never heard before. It felt like one of the longest nights, as if it was a whole year.

Our voices. Our stories.

In the morning, we left our house to see half the town destroyed and hundreds of people dead from the intense shelling. 12 of our relatives were corpses ...they were dead without souls ...

Due to the severe fear that I felt after seeing the killing and death scenes, I lost 90% of my vision, and I could not see well. It was an indescribable fear... after that incident, I couldn't read or learn. I was like a blind person.

My family started looking for a treatment to help my vision return. I traveled from one area to another with my father and grandfather, looking for a doctor. After several days, we finally found a doctor, but when he examined me, he said that he couldn't do anything. He asked for imaging and lab studies, but there was not a single hospital functioning because all hospitals were shelled.

The only option left for my father was to go to Turkey for treatment. I remember that day was one of the most difficult ones. My family and I entered the Turkish land, running in the dark. I heard bullets shooting and my sibilings crying. I didn't see anything except for some sunlight...

We crossed the borders and we reached Istanbul.

My father rented an empty house without carpets or a fireplace. There were no mattresses or anthing else in that house. It was winter time, and the snow was covering the wide city. My father didn't have enough money to buy food, covers, or anything to furnish the house, so we felt the severe cold for several days.

Some Turkish people knocked on our house, carrying some furniture for us. They were of the best people amongst us. We got to know a Turkish lady. She went with my mother to the hospital because my mother didn't know any Turkish. After several months and after seeing the lab results, my doctor said that there was no treatment for my eyes.

Our voices. Our stories.

He said that I had to go to school. I had psychiatric therapy for a year. With the help of our Turkish brothers, I learned the Turkish language and I'm in fifth grade now.

We sometimes face some racism like when my siblings and I were playing during Eid and a lady said, "Go back to Syria. You have destroyed your country and now you want to destroy Turkey." I didn't know how to answer, so I smiled and entered the house. We face expensive prices and expensive rents every day. My family has 6 people, and we live in a small house … but our dreams make it big.

I will fulfill my dream when I grow up. I'm going to be a leader, who protects my country and helps the poor and the needy. Even today, I don't understand why wars exist? What fault did I do to lose my vision? What's the fault of all the kids who died? One day, my vision may come back, and we will go back to our country and to our big house. This is my hope...

Our voices. Our stories.

طليحة

ما زلت أذكر صوت قنابل الطائرات. يوماً ما قررنا الذهاب إلى تركيا. لم يكن سهلاً الذهاب إليها. في عام 2015، عشنا في منزل صغير في فاتح، المنزل كان في حالة سيئة، ولكن بقينا فيه لمدة ستة أشهر قبل أن نقرّر العودة إلى سورية بسبب سوء وضعنا المالي. رجعنا إلى قريتنا لمدة سنة واحدة ولكنها بالنسبة لي كانت كأنها مائة سنة قد مرّت بس الطائرات والقنابل العشوائية، لقد كانت لحظات مخيفة لا أريد التحدث عنها مرة أخرى.

ساءت الأوضاع. بشكل غير متوقع، أخبرنا والدي أنه علينا الرحيل. كان علينا حزم أمتعتنا في ليلة والمغادرة بهدوء. عُثِرَ علينا عندما غادرنا، وبعدها قاموا بحبسنا في ملعب لكرة السلة. حاولنا المغادرة مراتٍ عديدة، ولكنهم كانوا يقبضون علينا في كل مرة. في أحد المرات، كان علينا عبور الغابة لتجاوز الحدود: كانت مظلمة، وهادئة. كان بإمكاننا فقط سماع صوت الأفاعي والأشجار. في ذلك اليوم، أختي اعتقدت أننا ميّتون بسبب الحفر الكبيرة، أختي لم تكن قادرة على رؤيتهم في الظلام واعتقدت أننا سنسقط في احداها.

تركنا نصف أملاكنا لأنه لم يكن ممكناً حملهم معنا. قرّرنا السفر متفرّقين. أولاً، ذهب أخواي لوحدهما. غادرت أختي لوحدها بعدهم. أختي كانت حوالي عشر سنين عندما تجاوزت حدود تركيا. كانت خائفة جداً. الآن فقط أمي وأخي بقيا لوحدهما. عانت أمي لألامٍ في قدميها.

Our voices. Our stories.

انتقلنا إلى مكان يدعى بلاط في عام 2016، كان عليّ أن أبدأ المدرسة في ذلك الوقت. درست لمدة سنتين، بعدها جئنا إلى فاتح وبدأت مدرسة أخرى. أتممت التعليم الثانوي هناك، ولكن بعد ذلك، كوفيد بدأ الانتشار. لو بقينا في سورية، حالنا كان لربّما أسوأ. بدأنا نلاحظ العنصرية، ولكن بالطبع هناك أناس آخرون قد ساعدونا وقت قدومنا. لهؤلاء الناس، أقول شكراً جزيلاً.

Taliha - Curious

I can still remember the sounds of plane bombs. We decided to go to Turkey one day. It wasn't easy. In 2015, we lived in a small house in Fatih. The house was in bad shape, but we stayed for about 6 months before deciding to return to Syria because of our poor financial situation. We went back to the village where we lived 1 year ago, but for me it was as if 100 years had passed because bombs from planes were being dropped randomly. It was such a frightening moment that I don't even want to talk about it again.

Things got worse. Unexpectedly, my father informed us that we had to leave. We had to pack our belongings in one night and leave quietly. We were caught when we left, and they locked us up in a basketball court. We tried to go many times, but we were always caught. Finally, one day we crossed a forest to cross the border: it was dark, there was silence. We could only hear the sounds of snakes and trees. That day my sister thought we would die because there were big potholes, and my sister did not see them in the dark and would fall down.

Our voices. Our stories.

We had left half of our belongings because it was not possible to carry them around. We decided to travel separately. First, my 2 brothers went alone. After my brothers left, my sister had to go out alone. My sister was about 10 years old when she crossed the borders of Turkey. She was very scared. Now, only my mother and brother were left behind. My mother had a hard time because her feet were always sore.

We moved to a place called Balat in 2016. I had to start school at that time. I studied for 2 years, but then we came to Fatih and I started at a different school. I finished secondary school there, but then, COVID-19 spread. If we had stayed in Syria, our situation would have gotten worse. We started to see racism but of course others helped us when we first arrived. To them, I say thank you very much.

منيرة

انا طفلة في العاشرة من عمري... كبرت وتربيت في احضان أسرة متواضعه... مع ابي وامي واخي... كنا نعيش في قرية يسودها الحب والأمان... وأجمل ما فيها جدي الحنون وجدتي العطوفة التي كنت كلما أتردد إلى دارهم أشعر بالدفئ والحنان ولا أنسى موائد الطعام التي كانت تصنع لأجلي.

إلى أن جاء ذلك اليوم الذي قررنا فيه أن نخرج من عتمة الظلام الى نور الحرية... فخرج والدي مع مجموعة من الشبان ليطالبو بحياة كريمة كما وعدني... فعندما وعيت وصرت أحس بهذه الحياة فقدت اغلى ما في الوجود فخرج والدي ولم يعد...
نعم استشهد والدي وانا في الرابعة من عمري. لم اكتفي من حنانه بما يكفي كنت دائما اشتاق له لكي يحملني كلما ابكي ويمسح دموعي...

رحل ابي ورحلت معه رائحة الحياة وهو يدافع من أجل أن ينير لي طريق الحرية... فتركني يتيمة أنظر إلى الحياة وأنا حزينة... فكانت والدتي تحاول أن تكون لي الأب الذي لم أرتوي من عطائه بما يكفي والأم الحنونة التي تمسك بيدي لنخوض معركة الحياة معا... فتركت بيتنا الدافئ وتركت كتبي واصدقائي وتركت اغلى مافي الوجود وهو قبر أبي الذي كنت أزوره أنا وأمي وأخي عندما كنا نشتاق له ونضع الياسمين على قبره ونحدثه كما لو أنه بجانبنا... أخرجونا من ديارنا إلى مدينة إدلب الخضراء ولكنها لم تكن خضراء كما كنا نظن فلم

نعثر فيها على الأمان ولم نعثر على أية أبواب مفتوحة سوى باب الله وأبواب دولة تركيا التي عثرنا فيها على الأمان بعيداً عن الظلم والجوع والحرب فمن حقي أن أعيش كباقي أطفال العالم وأحقق حلم أبي وأمي بأن أصبح دكتورة المستقبل لأعالج كل طفل تألم من ويلات الحروب واخيراً أطلب من الله أن يعيدنا إلى بلادنا منصورين رافعين رؤوسنا لأشم ترابها وأقبل ثرى أبي الغالي... شكراً تركيا... شكراً رجب طيب اردوغان... الفتاة الفاقدة لأغلى ما لديها.

Munira - Full of Light

I am a 10 year old girl... I was born and raised in a poor family with my father, mother and brother. We used to live in a village full of love and safety ... my best memories were of my caring grandfather and my loving grandmother.

I used to feel warmth and kindness every time I visited them. I can't forget all the food that was made for me, until that day came when we decided to leave the darkness to a bright freedom. My father went out with some other guys demanding a decent life as he promised me. As I grew up and matured, I started feeling that this life has lost the most precious thing. My father left but he never came back. Yes, he became a martyr when I was 4 years old... I didn't have enough of his kindness. I have always missed him. I missed how he used to carry me when I cried and then wiped my tears.

My father left, and the smell of life left with him. He was defending to light the path of freedom for us, but he left me as

Our voices. Our stories.

an orphan who looks at this life with sad eyes. My mother was trying to be like a father too ... the father whose giving I missed. She was the caring mother who held my hand as we fought the battle of life together.

I left our warm house ... I left my books and my friends ... and I left the most precious thing in the world, my father's grave. I used to visit that grave with my mother and brother whenever I missed him. I used to place jasmine roses over it, and we used to talk to him as if he were beside us...

They forced us out to the green city of Idlib, however, it was not as green as we thought because we didn't find safety and we didn't find any open doors except for the door to Allah [God], and the doors to Turkey where we found safety far away from the oppression, the hunger, and the war.

It is my right to live like the rest of the children around the world, and to fulfill my parents' dream of becoming a doctor to treat every child who suffered from all wars. Finally, I ask Allah [God]

116

to help us return to our homeland, victorious with our heads held high … to smell its sands and to kiss my father's grave. Thank you Turkey … thank you Rajab Tayyab Erdogan … for helping the girl who left the most precious things she owned.

Our voices. Our stories.

ماهر

في بداية الحرب كنت في عامي الثامن من العمر نعيش حياة جميلة ومريحة مع عائلتي لدي غرفتي أتشاركها مع أخي الأكبر. بيتنا واسع وجميل... لم أفهم لماذا بدأت الصواريخ والقذائف تهطل فوق منازلنا. كنت أركض الى بيت جدتي في الطابق الأول لأنه أكثر أمانا كما كانت أمي تقول لنا... في أحد الأيام سقطت قذيفة في المدرسة وكنا في الصف بدرس اللغة العربية وأصبح الجميع يصرخ ويبكي وقفت وحدي انتظر أمي لأنها وعدتني بأنها ستكون موجودة لحمايتي دائماً... رأيت أمي تركض لتحملني رغم ثقل وزني.

عشنا دون كهرباء أو ماء أو طعام يكفي الجميع. كانت أمي وأبي يأكلون القليل فقط لنشبع أنا وأخوتي لأن الطعام لم يكن كافيا أبدا قاومنا الموت تحت القصف والمدافع لشهور قبل أن يدخل أبي المنزل ويقول لنا هيا حان وقت الرحيل... تركنا منزلنا وذكرياتنا وأحلامنا وخرجنا نحمل بعض الحاجيات الضرورية تركنا خلفنا المدرسة والمنزل واحلامنا الجميلة... عشنا في المدينة تحت سيطرة جنود النظام لثلاث سنوات بظروف قاسية ولكن إصرار أمي على تعليمنا وأكمال دراستنا في المدارس جعلنا من المتفوقين رغم الظروف الصعبة...

حتى بدأ الجنود يأخذون الرجال للحرب أو للقتل... قالت أمي نحن بخير ما دمنا معاً سنكون يداً من خمس أصابع نقبض على بعضنا

لنواجه الخطر والموت... ثم في إحدى الليالي دخل الجنود منزلنا المستأجر ليحقق مع أبي لأنه من الغوطة. بعد ذلك أطلقوا سراحه وقررت عائلتي السفر لأوروبا... اخذنا جواز السفر وتركنا الوطن باتجاه تركيا اسطنبول. هناك كانت الحياة صعبة ونحن نحاول الخروج باتجاه أوروبا عبر الغابات في ليالي الشتاء الباردة كنا نمشي بالغابة وأنا ممسك بيد أمي خائفا من العتمة والبرد والطين في قلب ظلمات الغابات.

وعندما وصلنا لليونان بدأ الجنود بضرب الأطفال والناس لأنهم سوريين ولاجئين ثم اعتقلونا وأرجعونا عبر الغابة لضفة النهر على الجانب التركي بعد ان مشينا ثلاثة أيام في الغابة... جلس الناس يبكون فقالت لنا أمي نحن بخير لأننا معاً إذا أراد الله أن نبقى في تركيا فسنكون كالنباتات تضرب جذورها بالأرض لتزهر رغم الشتاء والثلج أمسكنا أيدي بعضنا وعدنا مع الجنود الأتراك الذين كانوا لطفاء معنا وأعطونا طعامهم لنأكل بعد كل التعب والعناء... عدنا لإسطنبول واستأجرنا منزلاً وبدأ أبي وأمي بالعمل.

ودخلنا المدارس وبدأنا تعلم اللغة التركية... وتجاوزنا كل الصعوبات لأننا مع بعضنا عائلة قوية والآن أختي في الجامعة تدرس الهندسة الوراثية والعلوم و أخي الأكبر يدرس أيضاً أول سنة بالجامعة وأنا أحضر امتحان القبول لأدخل الجامعة وحلمي أن أدرس هندسة الحاسوب... نحن كأزهار الياسمين في دمشق سنزهر أينما كنا ما دمنا معاً... هكذا قالت أمي وأنا أصدقها دائما.

120

Mahir - Skillful

When the war began, I was 8 years old living a beautiful and comfortable life with my family. I had my own room, which I shared with my brother. Our house was big and beautiful. I didn't understand why rockets and bombs were dropping over our homes. I used to run to my grandmother's house which was on the first floor because it was safer as my mother used to say...

One day, a bomb was dropped during school, and we were in Arabic class. Everyone started crying and shouting. I stood alone waiting for my mother because she promised me that she would always be there to protect me.. I saw my mother running to carry me despite my heavy weight.

We lived without electricity or water or enough food for everyone ... My parents used to eat very little so that my brothers and I could eat because the food was not enough for everyone. We resisted death under the bombing and shooting for months before my father entered the house and told us it was time to leave. We left our home, our memories, and our dreams, leaving with only some necessary items. We left behind our school, our houses, and our beautiful dreams …

We lived in the city under the regime control for 3 years. We lived in a bad situation, however, my mother insisted that we continue our education at school, so we would be amongst the outstanding students, despite the difficult situations.

Even when the soldiers started taking men to war or to death, my mother said, "we're ok as long as we stick together. We're going to be like a hand with five fingers, holding each other in the face of danger and death." Then, one night, soldiers entered our rental house to investigate my father because he was from Al-Ghouta. When they released him, my family decided to travel to Europe. We took our passports, and we left our homeland towards Istanbul, Turkey. Life was difficult as we tried to escape to Europe through the forests during the cold winter nights. While we were walking in the forest, I held my mother's hand because I was afraid of the darkness, the cold, and the mud inside those dark forests.

When we arrived in Greece, the soldiers started to hit the children and the people because they were Syrian refugees. Then they arrested us and forced us to go back through the forest to the Turkish side of the river after we walked for 3 days in the forest. People sat and cried, but then my mother said, "we're ok because Allah [God] is with us. If Allah [God] wants us to stay in Turkey, then we will be like plants with roots spreading in the ground to flower despite the winter and the snow. We held each other's hands and went back with Turkish soldiers who were very nice to us and gave us their food to eat after all our exhaustion and suffering. When we went back to Istanbul, we rented a house, and my father and mother started to work.

We started school and learned Turkish … we passed all these difficulties because we were a strong family. Now, my sister is in college studying genetic engineering and biology, my eldest brother is in his first year in college, and I'm preparing for the acceptance exam to enter the college. My dream is to study computer engineering. We are like jasmine roses of Damascus, we will flower whenever we are together. That's what my mom said and I always believe her.

عظيما

كانت أياماً صعبة وذكرياتها مؤلمة.

أول أيام الحرب كنت صغيرة لا أستطيع التذكر جيداً. لكن هناك مواقف لا أستطيع نسيانها كيوم حصول الانفجار كنا نسمع صوته القوي المخيف المرعب وكنت أركض لحضن أمي او أبي وأرتجف خوفاً وعند قدوم رجال الأمن كانوا يضربون على الأبوب بشكل مخيف مرعب لتفتيش المنازل... أخذوا الرجال للتحقيق. خفت عندما أخذو أبي للتحقق من هويته.

وبعدة أيام قضيناها في فترة الحرب بدون كهرباء أو ماء أو ما يكفي من الطعام قرر أبي أن يسافر إلى تركيا وحده ليعمل وتركنا في سوريا.

كان هذا القرار صعباً ولم أرغب بترك أبي. لكنه ذهب وبقينا ننتظره لعامين ولم تنته الحرب فكان علينا ان نسافر أيضا للعيش مع أبي في تركيا لكن لا يوجد طريق لنصل عنده سوى التهريب غير القانوني.

الخطوة الأولى كانت أن نذهب إلى إدلب أنا وأمي وإخوتي الصغار. بقينا ننتظر في قرية صغيرة على أطراف إدلب لنتمكن من محاولة الدخول عبر الطرق المخفية في الجبال باتجاه تركيا. فلم يكن هناك إمكانية للسفر بطريقة نظامية رغم امتلاكنا لجواز السفر الرسمي. كان الأمر مخيفاً متعباً للغاية كنت

125

Our voices. Our stories.

أرى أمي متعبة وأخوتي الصغار نيام بفعل الأدوية المنومة التي أعطاها المهرب لهم كي لا يصدروا أي ضجيج ونحن نتسلل للأراضي التركية.

حاولنا العبور لأكثر من عشرة مرات وفي كل مرة كانت الجندرما التركية تمسك بنا وتعيدنا الى ادلب فالعبور ممنوع. في بعض المرات أطلقوا الرصاص في الهواء لإخافة الناس من الوصول إلى أراضيهم وفي آخر مرة عبرنا ونجحنا من دخول تركيا وكان أبي بانتظارنا. كانت فرحة عظيمة أن أرى أبي وأصل لمكان لا يوجد فيه أصوات قنابل ولا رصاص ولا خوف من أن ندفن أحياء تحت الركام. ولكن عاد أبي إلى اسطنبول وبقينا في ولاية أخرى.

على الحدود ننتظر أن يجمع بعض المال لأخذنا فهو لا يملك أموال الحجز للطريق ولا منزلاً نعيش فيه معه هناك فكان عليه أن يعمل ليوفر المال لمدة أربع شهور تقريباً. أول ما قامت به أمي أنها استخرجت لنا الهويات وقامت بتسجيلنا في المدارس وكم كانت اللغة الجديدة صعبة علينا فالجميع يتحدث لغة لا نعرفها. حاولت التعلم والآن أجيد اللغة التركية بشكل مقبول.

جمع أبي المال وانتقلنا للعيش معه في اسطنبول والآن أنا سعيدة وسأكمل تعليمي لأصبح معلمة فأنا أحب الأطفال... ولكن هناك حزن شديد في قلبي على وطني والأهل فيه وأتمنى من كل قلبي أن ترتاح قلوب الناس في سوريا ويعود لوطن لأفضل حال.

126

Azeema - Determined

They were difficult days with bad memories. During the first days of war, I was a young girl, so I can't remember very well. However, there are moments I can't forget like the day of the big explosion. We used to hear its frightening, loud noise when I ran to my mother's or father's lap and was shaking with fear. When the secret men came, they knocked on the doors in a scary way to search the houses... they took the men for investigation. I was scared when they took my father to investigate his identity.

After some time during the war without electricity, water, or enough food, my father decided to travel to Turkey alone to work there. He left us in Syria. It was a difficult decision and I didn't want to leave my father. However, he left and we patiently waited for him for 2 years. The war didn't end, so we had to travel to live with my father in Turkey, but there was no way to reach him without illegal smuggling.

Our voices. Our stories.

The first step was to go to Idlib with my mother and my younger siblings. We stayed in a small village on the outskirts of Idlib, trying to enter through the hidden routes in the mountains towards Turkey. We couldn't afford to travel legally even though we had official passports. It was scary and very exhausting to see my mother tired and my younger siblings sleeping after taking sedative drugs that the smuggler gave us, so we would not make any noise while we were escaping into Turkey.

We tried to pass through about 10 times, but each time the Gendarmerie force of Turkey arrested us and brought us back to Idlib. Passing the border was forbidden. Sometimes they shot fire in the air to scare people from passing to their lands. However, during our last attempt, we succeeded and entered Turkey. My father was waiting for us. It was a great pleasure to see my father and to reach a place without the sound of bombing or shooting. I was no longer scared of being buried alive under the rubble.

Our voices. Our stories.

However my father returned to Istanbul, and we stayed in a different state on the border waiting for him to gather some money to take us because he didn't have enough money for the road or a house for us to live with him. He worked for about four months to save enough money. Meanwhile, the first thing my mother did was get us IDs and register us at schools. The new language was very difficult for us. Everyone was talking a language we didn't know. I tried to learn and now I adequately know Turkish.

My father gathered money. We moved to live with him in Istanbul. Now I'm happy and I will continue my education to become a teacher because I love children... however there's a intense sadness in my heart for my country and the people there. I hope from the bottom of my heart that Syrian peoples' hearts find ease and that my country may be in the best situation.

Our voices. Our stories.

Our voices. Our stories.

جاسرة

الغيوم السوداء.

عمري خمس عشرة سنة، أنا من سورية. كما تعلمي، هناك حرب في سورية. خلال عيشي هناك، كنّا دائماً ننتقل من مدينة إلى أخرى. عندما بدأت الحرب، كنّا في وضع سيّئٍ جداً... كنا خائفين جداً. بعدها، قرّرنا القدوم إلى تركيا، ولكن والدي رفض ذلك. جئنا إلى تركيا بسهولة واستقررنا في منزل. كان لديّ أخّين أكبر مني: كانوا صغاراً، ولكن كان يجب عليهم العمل.

لدينا أقرباء في تركيا، عموم وعمّات، إلا أنهم لم يساعدونا. في ذلك الوقت، كنت في التاسعة من عمري. كان يتوجّب علينا الذهاب إلى المدرسة، ولكن لم نكن نعرف اللغة التركية. أقاربنا يتحدّثون التركية ولكنهم لم يساعدونا، لهذا السبب كنّا نشاهد بحسرة بينما باقي الأطفال في المدرسة. لاحقاً، بعد عدة أشهر، لم يتوجّب على إخوتي العمل ولم يتبقى معنا مال ولم يرسل والدي المال.

استسلمنا ورجعنا إلى القرية حيث كان يعيش والدي مع زوجته، ولكن والدي خسر عمله بعد فترةٍ قصيرة. استنفدنا جميع أموالنا، لإن والدي لم يعمل لمدة سنةً كاملة، ثم بعد سنتين، قال: احزموا أمتعتكم، نحن مغادرون. تجهزنا للسفر في المساء، ركبنا السيارة، ثم بقينا في القرية مع صديق والدي بالقرب من تركيا.

131

الرجل كان مهرّباً، شخص يأخذ الناس من سورية إلى تركيا بعد حصوله على المال. حاولنا القدوم إلى لتركيا لمدة شهرين، ولكن فشلنا. بعدها قال والدي: دعونا نذهب متفرقين. أولاً، ذهب أخوتي، ثم ذهبت أختي مع أخ آخر. رغبت البقاء مع أمي، ولكن اضطررت الذهاب وحيداً. بالطبع لم تكن سهلة. كنت أمسك يد شخص لم أعرفه بينما كنا نمشي في ظلام الليل. كنت خائفاً جداً.

بعد قدومي إلى تركيا، وصل أبي وأمي وزوجة أبي وأطفالها. بقينا مع عمّي لفترة حتى وجدنا منزلاً. إخوتي كانوا أكبر عمراً، لذلك كانوا قادرين على العمل. وضعنا تحسّن تدريجياً وكنا قادرين على العودة إلى المدرسة. الآن، في عام 2021، نعيش في منزلنا الخاص وأنا سعيد جداً. أتمنى أن أصبح جراحاً تجميلياً وأن أمتلك مستشفى خاصاً.

Jasira - Bold

DARK CLOUDS

I am 15 years old, and I am from Syria. As you know, there is war in Syria. When I lived there, we always moved from city to city. When the war started, we were in a very bad shape … we were very afraid. Then, we decided to come to Turkey, but my father did not want to come with us. We came to Turkey easily and settled in a house. I had two older brothers: They were both very small, but they had to work.

We have relatives in Turkey, uncles and aunts, but none of them could help us. I was 9 years old at that time. We had to go to school, but we could not speak Turkish. Our relatives knew Turkish, but they never helped us, so we watched sadly while their children went to school. Soon, after a few months, my brothers did not have work and we did not have any money and my father would not send us money.

We gave in and we went back to the village where my father lived with his second wife, but my father soon became unemployed. Because he didn't work for a year, we started to run out of money, and two years later, he said, "Pack up, you're leaving." We got ready in the evening, got into a car, and stayed in a village close to Turkey with my father's friend.

The man was a smuggler, a person who takes people from Syria to Turkey after receiving money. We tried to come to Turkey for two months, but it didn't happen. Then my father said, "let's go separately." First, my first two brothers went, then my sister and my other brother left. I wanted to stay with my mother, but then I had to go to Turkey myself. Of course, it was not easy. I was holding the hand of a person I did not know while walking in the dark at night. I was very afraid.

After I came to Turkey, my father, mother, and father's second wife and children arrived. We stayed with my uncle for a while until we found a house. My brothers were older, so they could work properly now. Our situation gradually improved and then we could go to school. Now, in 2021, we live in our own house and I am very happy. I hope to become a plastic surgeon and have my own hospital.

Our voices. Our stories.

What is my biggest
dream?

What is My Biggest Dream?

What is my biggest dream?

Recapturing our Childhood

Shuja – Boy, Age 15

Hazeem – Boy, Age 20

Jehaan – Girl, Age 13

Ameed – Boy, Age 14

Farrah – Girl, Age 13

Raja – Girl, Age 12

Taliha – Girl, Age 13

Munira – Girl, Age 10

Mahir – Boy, Age 17

Azeema – Girl, Age 11

Aqsa – Girl, Age 12

Iman – Girl, Age 12

What is my biggest dream?

شجا

حلمي الكبير وهدفي أريد أن
أعود إلى سورية، البلد اللتي
بدأت فيها حياتي مع أصدقائي
والناس الذين أحبهم

What is my biggest dream?

Shuja - Brave

My biggest dream and goal I hope to achieve is to return to Syria, the country where I started my life with my friends and the people I love

What is my biggest dream?

هزيم

لأتعلم أكثر من عشر لغات، أكمل جامعتي و أصبح رجل أعمال ناجح

What is my biggest dream?

Hazeem - Intelligent

To learn more than 10 languages, finish my university, and be a successful businessman

What is my biggest dream?

جيهان

حلمي الكبير ان اكون رسامة
كبيرة وامي إلى جانبي

What is my biggest dream?

Jehaan - Creative

My big dream is to be a great artist with my mom by my side

What is my biggest
dream?

عميد

حلمي أن أكون قائدا احمى
وطني واساعد الفقراء
والمساكين

145

What is my biggest dream?

Ameed - Leader

My dream is to be a leader to protect my country and help the poor and needy

What is my biggest dream?

فَرَح

أريد أن أساعد الناس بالسماع لهم

What is my biggest dream?

Farrah - Happiness

I want to help everyone by listening to them

رجاء

أريد منزلا كبيرا، أن أصبح غنيا، أن تكون لدي حديقة واسعة ولمساعدة الآخرين

ABC

What is my biggest dream?

ABC

ABC

Raja - Hope

ABC

ABC

ABC

I want a big house, a big garden, and to be rich and help people

ABC

ABC

ABC

ABC

ABC

ABC

What is my biggest dream?

طليحة

أريد أن أذهب إلى الولايات المتحدة الامريكية و إلى كوريا لأنني أحب شعبيهما

What is my biggest dream?

Taliha - Curious

I want to go to the USA and Korea to live there because I love Korean and American people

What is my biggest dream?

منيرة

هدفي أن أكمل دراستي
واعيش بسلام

What is my biggest dream?

Munira - Full of Light

My goal is to continue my studies and live in peace

What is my biggest dream?

ماهر

هدفي الأكبر أن أقدر على صنع مشروعي الخاص عندما أكبر

What is my biggest dream?

Mahir - Skillful

My biggest goal is to make my own engineering project when I'm older

What is my biggest dream?

عظيما

اهدفي اتعلم وحلمي اني نضل
بخير وكيد بتمنى ضل بجانب
عيلتي امي و ابي واخواتي
نظلّ. وأكيد أتنمى أظل

What is my biggest dream?

Azeema - Determined

My goal is to study, and my dream is to stay healthy. As I grow up, I hope to stay close to my family: my mom, dad, and my sisters

What is my biggest dream?

أقسى

نحن نحلم بأن نعيش في بلد شعبه يحبنا ونتأقلم عليه

What is my biggest dream?

Aqsa - Intelligent

We dream of living in a country where its people love us and to get used to the country

What is my biggest dream?

إِيمَان

حلمي ان أكون مغنية
مشهورة.
أريد أن أترك أثر إيجابي
على العالم وأن أكون
شخصاً محبّاً وأن أساعد
الناس وأن أعطي المال
للفقراء

What is my biggest dream?

Iman - Faith

My dream is to be a famous singer. I also want to make a positive impact on the world, be a loving person, and help people by giving money to the poor

What would my life be
like if I weren't a
refugee?

What Would My Life Be Like if I Weren't a Refugee?

What would my life be like if I weren't a refugee?

Recapturing our Childhood

Shuja – Boy, Age 15

Hazeem – Boy, Age 20

Jehaan – Girl, Age 13

Ameed – Boy, Age 14

Farrah – Girl, Age 13

Raja – Girl, Age 12

Taliha – Girl, Age 13

Munira – Girl, Age 10

Mahir – Boy, Age 17

Azeema – Girl, Age 11

Aqsa – Girl, Age 12

Iman – Girl, Age 12

What would my life be like if I weren't a refugee?

شجا

كنت لم أشعر بمعنى الخوف،
كنت لم أعرف معنى الجوع،
كنت لم أعرف معنى خسارة
أشياء ثمينة. أنا متأكد أنَّ ما
حصل لي كان مُجرَّد درسٍ في
الحياة وهو نعمةٌ بالنسبة لي

What would my life be like if I weren't a refugee?

Shuja - Brave

I would not know the meaning of fear ... I would not know the meaning of hunger ... I would not know the meaning of losing precious things. I am sure that what happened to me is just a lesson in this life and it is a blessing for me

What would my life be like if I weren't a refugee?

هزيم

حياتي كانت ستكون أسهل
وأفضل، كنت سأصنع مستقبلاً
أفضل

What would my life be like if I weren't a refugee?

Hazeem - Intelligent

My life would be easier and better, and I could make a better future

What would my life be like if I weren't a refugee?

جيهان

سنشعر بالاستقرار لو لم نكن لاجئين

What would my life be like if I weren't a refugee?

Jehaan - Creative

We would feel more secure if we weren't refugees

What would my life be like if I weren't a refugee?

عميد

سوف يصبح كل شئ أجمل

What would my life be like if I weren't a refugee?

Ameed - Leader

Everything would be more beautiful

What would my life be
like if I weren't a
refugee?

فَرَح

كان من الممكن أن أكون
أكثر سعادة وأن أرى
جدّي، وعمّي، وباقي أهلي

What would my life be like if I weren't a refugee?

Farrah - Happiness

I would be very happy, and I would see my grandfather, grandmother, uncles, and the rest of my extended family

What would my life be like if I weren't a refugee?

رجاء

سأكون سعيدا جدا

175

What would my life be like if I weren't a refugee?

Raja - Hope

I would be very happy

What would my life be like if I weren't a refugee?

طليحة

إذًا لم أكن لاجئاً، كنت قد ذهبت إلى أي بلدٍ أريد لأنَّ اللاجئين لا يستطيعون الذهاب إلى أيّة بلد آخر

What would my life be like if I weren't a refugee?

Taliha - Curious

If I weren't a refugee, I could go to any country I want because refugees cannot go into other countries

What would my life be like if I weren't a refugee?

منيرة

سأكون في بيتي... في ارضي... سأكون مع أقاربي واصدقائي اشاركهم الافراح والأحزان

What would my life be like if I weren't a refugee?

Munira - Full of Light

I would be home ... in my land ... I would be with my relatives and friends sharing their joys and sorrows

What would my life be like if I weren't a refugee?

ماهر

كان يمكن أن أكون الأفضل لأنّني كنت قد عشت في منزلنا ومع أربائي. كنت قد تعلّمت بلغتي ولم أُعامل كلاجئ. الحياة قد تكون أسهل وأكثر راحةً

What would my life be like if I weren't a refugee?

Mahir - Skillful

It would have been perfect because I would have lived in our house, I would have seen my relatives, and I would have been able to study in my language. I would not have been treated as a refugee. Life would have been easier and more comfortable

What would my life be like if I weren't a refugee?

عظيما

انا متأكدة بأنها ستكون حياة جميلة لأني ببلدي

What would my life be like if I weren't a refugee?

Azeema - Determined

I am sure it would be a beautiful life because I would be in my homeland

What would my life be like if I weren't a refugee?

أقسى

ليس مهم ان تكون ببلد غير الذي كنت تعيش به اللمهم ان نتأقلم مع البيئة والناس

What would my life be like if I weren't a refugee?

Aqsa - Intelligent

It's not important to be in a different country other than your own country. The important thing is to get used to the environment and people

What would my life be like if I weren't a refugee?

إِيمَان

كنت سأرى عائلتي وكنت قد عشت بسلام بين أقربائي. في تركيا يوجد فقط أمي وأبي وأخي وأختي. في العراق، أقرباؤنا مسيحيون، لذلك يعيشون بسلام، ولكن نحن مسلمون، لذلك نحن في خطر. سُجِنَ والدي عندما كان صغيراً بسبب قراءة القرآن

What would my life be like if I weren't a refugee?

Iman - Faith

I would have seen my family and lived in peace amongst my relatives because it is just my mother, father, brother, and sister in Turkey. Because in Iraq, our relatives are Christian, they live in peace, but we are Muslim, so we are at risk. When my father was younger, he was imprisoned for reading the Quran

What is one message I
want to share with you?

What is One Message I Want to Share With You?

What is one message I want to share with you?

Recapturing our Childhood

Shuja – Boy, Age 15

Hazeem – Boy, Age 20

Jehaan – Girl, Age 13

Ameed – Boy, Age 14

Farrah – Girl, Age 13

Taliha – Girl, Age 13

Munira – Girl, Age 10

Mahir – Boy, Age 17

Azeema – Girl, Age 11

Aqsa – Girl, Age 12

Iman – Girl, Age 12

What is one message I
want to share with you?

شجا

لا يوجد جبل بلا قاع، ولا
قاع بلا قمة، وسوف نكون
في القمة قريباً

Shuja - Brave

There is no mountain without
a bottom, and there is no
bottom without a top, and we
will be at the top soon

What is one message I want to share with you?

هزيم

نحن لسنا لاجئين. الله فقط
أراد أن ينشر الياسمين في
العالم

What is one message I want to share with you?

Hazeem - Intelligent

We are not refugees. God only wanted jasmine to spread in the world

What is one message I want to share with you?

جيهان وأقسى

نحن بوضعنا الحالي لا يأثر على مستقبلنا اي شئ نتمنى أن نحقق اهدافنا بالحياة

What is one message I want to share with you?

Jehaan - Creative and Aqsa - Intelligent

Our current situation doesn't affect our future. We hope to achieve our goals in life

What is one message I want to share with you?

عميد

اريد ان اقول للعالم لماذا الظلم ولماذا الحرب ولماذا العنصرية؟

نحن بشر ولن نبقى على هذه الأرض.

افعل الخير في جميع الأوقات والأماكن

What is one message I want to share with you?

Ameed - Leader

I want to tell the world why oppression, why war, and why racism?
We are all human and will not stay on this earth forever.
Always do good in all places

فَرَح

إريد أن تتوقف الحروب
ليعيش الجميع بسعادة

What is one message I want to share with you?

Farrah - Happiness

I want wars to end and for everyone to live happily

What is one message I want to share with you?

طليحة

أوقفوا الحروب لأنها تؤثر
على عقل وجسد الناس. أنا
واحد من هؤلاء الناس. كما
يجب أن نمنح المرأة
جميع الحقوق

What is one message I want to share with you?

Taliha - Curious

Let wars end because they affect people physically and mentally. I am one of those people. We should also grant women all rights

منيرة

رسالتنا إلى المجتمع... ان
ينظرون إلينا باحترام و أننا
أناس لنا وطن ولنا كرامه
وان لا ينظرون إلينا نظرة
عنصرية.
نريد أن تنتهي الحرب ونعود
إلى شامنا... اشتقنا لعربيتنا

What is one message I want to share with you?

Munira - Full of Light

Our message to society is to look at us with respect as people who have a homeland, and dignity and not give us a racist look. We want the war to end, and we want to return to our Syria. We miss our Arab land

What is one message I want to share with you?

ماهر

لا يهم عرقك، أو لون
بشرتك، أو من أين أنت
لأننا جميعنا بشر

What is one message I want to share with you?

Mahir - Skillful

Your race, skin color, or where you are from doesn't matter because we are all human

What is one message I want to share with you?

عظيما

بدنا نكون بخير والله يفرجا
على بلدنا

What is one message I
want to share with you?

Azeema - Determined

We want to be good. May God
make it easy for our country

What is one message I want to share with you?

إِيمَان

اشكر البلد الذي ساعدنا في الحرب واستقبلنا بكل حب وطيبة

What is one message I want to share with you?

Iman - Faith

I thank the country that helped us during the war and welcomed us with love and kindness

What Does Sharing My Story Mean to Me?

What does sharing my story mean to me?

Recapturing our Childhood

Shuja – Boy, Age 15

Hazeem – Boy, Age 20

Jehaan – Girl, Age 13

Munira – Girl, Age 10

Mahir – Boy, Age 17

Azeema – Girl, Age 11

Aqsa – Girl, Age 12

Iman – Girl, Age 12

What does sharing my story mean to me?

شجا

هذه أول مرّة أشارك فيها
قصّتي وأنا سعيدٌ جداً
بمشاركتها معك

213

What does sharing my story mean to me?

Shuja - Brave

This is the first time I'm sharing my story with someone, and I'm so glad I shared it with you

What does sharing my story mean to me?

هزيم

أمرٌ عظيم أن شارك قصتي
مع أناسٍ رائعون مثلك

What does sharing my story mean to me?

Hazeem - Intelligent

It's great to share my story with a wonderful person like you

What does sharing my story mean to me?

جيهان وأقسى

نشعر بإحساس جميل عندما يكون لدينا أصدقاء كثر

What does sharing my story mean to me?

Jehaan - Creative and Aqsa - Intelligent

We feel good when we make a lot of friends

What does sharing my story mean to me?

منيرة

هذه اول مرة تمنح لنا
الفرصة بالتكلم عن ما بداخلنا
شكرا لك على هذه الفكرة
الجميله

What does sharing my story mean to me?

Munira - Full of Light

This is the first time we're allowed to talk about what's inside our hearts. Thank you for this beautiful idea

What does sharing my story mean to me?

ماهر

لأظهر للعالم أنني لا أستسلم عن أحلامي مهما كانت كبيرة وصعبة، وأنني في يومٍ ما سأحقق نجاحي والعالم سيشاهد ذلك

Mahir - Skillful

To show the world that I do not give up and do not give up on my dreams, no matter how big and difficult. One day I will achieve success, and the world will see it

What does sharing my story mean to me?

عظيما

لم اشاركها من قبل. كتير حبيت خل المشاركة. شكرا لكي لأنك قرأتي قصتي

What does sharing my story mean to me?

Azeema - Determined

I have not shared my story before. I prefer this so much. Thank you because you read my story

What does sharing my story mean to me?

إِيمَان

يوجد الكثير في قلوبنا

What does sharing my story mean to me?

Iman - Faith

There's a lot of things in our hearts ...

Summer Qureshi is the editor and illustrator of the book, "Unsilenced: Voices of Children Refugees." She completed this work as a 17-year-old high school senior at The Lawrenceville School in New Jersey. Using the school's Welles Award and with the support of The GiveLight Foundation, Summer designed and led storytelling workshops directly with refugee children internationally. In publishing these stories, she and her students hope others are reminded of our shared global responsibility to support refugee children trying to re-anchor their dreams.

Summer studied translation theory as an English Merrill Scholar and presented her TEDx Talk on the importance of authentic diversity, differentiating between quantitative and qualitative diversity. She has also spoken about improving leadership selection systems on Malcolm Gladwell's podcast episode, "The Powerball Revolution." At The Lawrenceville School, Summer has served on the Diversity Council and Religious Life Council Leadership Teams. She is a board member of the L10 News Channel, The Lawrenceville Historical Review, and Muse visual arts council. She is also the Co-Founder and Co-President of the Minority Advocacy for Racial and Religious Collaboration. Outside school, Summer works extensively on refugee education, supporting orphans in Morocco, Syrian and Iraqi refugee children in Turkey, and fundraising for Afghan refugees in America. In college, Summer hopes to continue building child refugee awareness through social justice efforts.

Made in the USA
Coppell, TX
17 April 2023

15739245R00136